NUNEATON
IN OLD PHOTOGRAPHS

NUNEATON
IN OLD PHOTOGRAPHS

COLLECTED BY

STEPHEN CLEWS & SUSAN VAUGHAN

ALAN SUTTON
1988

Alan Sutton Publishing Limited
Brunswick Road · Gloucester

First published 1988

British Library Cataloguing in Publication Data

Nuneaton in old photographs.
1. Warwickshire. Nuneaton, history.
I. Clews, Stephen   II. Vaughan, Susan.
942.4'83

ISBN 0-86299-496-9

Typesetting and origination by
Alan Sutton Publishing Limited
Printed in Great Britain
by WBC Print Limited

CONTENTS

It's not the miles you travel
but the PACE that kills in Nuneaton.

INTRODUCTION

Nuneaton is changing. This is a statement which, perhaps surprisingly, could have been applied with equal emphasis at almost any time in the last hundred years. In that period there has always been a new suburban development just completed or in prospect. Likewise there has always been a major new building just completed or being planned. Change in Nuneaton has a rather ruthless uncompromising character. It involves clearing away and starting again. Conversion is a form of change rarely encountered; demolition is the keyword.

The town has seen radical change in its industrial base; it is no longer a town of mills and pits. Accompanying this there has been radical social change. Improved housing, sanitation and education are all recorded in the photographs, as are the changes in the use people make of their leisure time. The rise and fall of the cinema and the virtual disappearance of pubs from the Market Place reflect this. The increase in motorised traffic has led to many alterations in the town's layout. In the 1930s Corporation Street and Newtown Road formed an early traffic relief scheme. Later on, Vicarage Street cut Riversley Park in two and isolated the Museum from the other municipal buildings. Later still, Roanne Ringway rode roughshod over the town plan, changed the flow of traffic and finally resolved the century-long conflict between pedestrians and vehicles in the town centre.

To capture the changing history of Nuneaton in all its aspects is a challenging and difficult task and we can only hope that we have managed to convey something of that history in this book. To some extent our selection of photographs has been dictated by availability. It has also been greatly enhanced by those who have responded to requests for help.

Nuneaton is fortunate to have been the home of some local photographers whose work has both quality and interest. The work of Clare Speight and F.R. Jones is well represented in this book. In the early years of this century postcards were big business and local views were popular. Cards relating to 'George Eliot Country' were numerous and we have included some of these in our collection.

Our thanks to all who helped us to compile this book are recorded in the acknowledgements. We hope that it will encourage readers to keep photographs (dated and labelled!) which might, in half a century's time, be wanted for another book like this one. We also hope that you will derive as much pleasure from reading this book as we did in compiling it.

SECTION ONE

Streets and Buildings

BIRD'S EYE VIEW OF NUNEATON.

AN AERIAL VIEW OF THE TOWN taken from the top of the Nuneaton Electricity Company works chimney which was located behind the present Council House. It is interesting to note all the open space in the background of this 1910 photograph. In the top right-hand corner is the ash track of the Newdegate Arms sports ground.

Valentines Series

Market Place, Nuneaton

Come down in time for Tea or sales yours with love Nel

THE MARKET PLACE at the turn of the century. The sign-board on the left is that of the White Swan which stood on this site from the eighteenth century until 1962.

THE MARKET PLACE early this century again, but looking the other way. The low twin gables on the left belong to the Peacock Inn, at one time an important coaching inn, which was rebuilt shortly after this.

THE MARKET PLACE IN 1934.

QUEENS ROAD IN 1949.

Gate Hotel, Nuneaton.

THE GATE HOTEL, a temperance establishment built by Reginald Stanley in 1898 on the corner of Abbey Gate. The interior was extremely luxurious and included an early form of central heating.

BRIDGE STREET shortly before the First World War. The sign hanging outside W.H. Smith is one of the company's early advertising boards, a few of which can still be seen. The shop on the extreme right is Lipton's, the tea and coffee merchant.

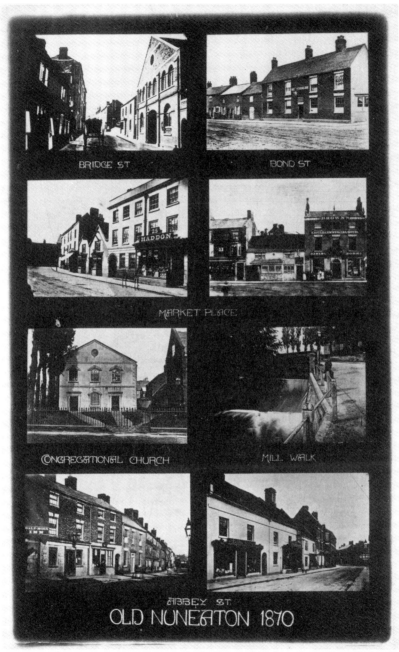

VIEWS OF NUNEATON, a composite postcard which could be bought in the 1900s, showing views of the town allegedly dating to 1870.

THE MARKET PLACE. The narrow entrance to the Market Place from Queens Road. The pub on the corner – The Crystal Palace – was demolished in 1909 to facilitate the road-widening scheme. The sale notices are fixed to the wall in this photograph which was taken shortly before demolition.

The Old Plough & Ball Inn, Abbey Green. Bradbury's Series No 11

THE PLOUGH AND BALL INN in Abbey Green, the pub's name being apparent from the sign outside. It was formerly called the Golden Ball. Thatched roofs were quite rare in Nuneaton by the late nineteenth century. The building to the right was probably a weaver's cottage with the large upstairs window providing light for working a hand-loom.

ABBEY GREEN. A view of Abbey Green at the turn of the century. In 1880 there was a report in the *Nuneaton Observer* that older inhabitants of the area still talked of Abbey Green as the site of a bull ring in the early nineteenth century.

ABBEY GREEN AND MIDLAND ROAD C. 1905. The horse-drawn vehicle outside the piano shop on the left is a Midland Railway parcel collection van.

ABBEY STREET IN 1870. On the right-hand side of the picture are several weavers' cottages, recognisable by the large upstairs windows. The family lived downstairs while the loom was housed on the top floor where the large window gave maximum light.

ABBEY STREET IN 1921.

ABBEY STREET, early this century, looking towards Abbey Green. The first two shops on the left are Jones (stationers) and Morse (draper and milliner) where window cleaning is in progress.

Nuneaton. I expect you know this view. Abbey Stre

ABBEY STREET C. 1908, looking towards Newdegate Street. Contrary to the comment on the postcard, few people now would recognise this view!

ABBEY STREET, looking towards Abbey Green in 1921. The new Scala cinema on the right-hand side was built in 1914.

BRIDGE STREET, a photograph taken possibly as early as 1870, showing the town's brewery on the right.

THE TOWN BRIDGE, Bridge Street, viewed from the river. During operations to improve the flow of water for the town mill, timbers of a former bridge are said to have been found beneath this.

COTON ROAD, NUNEATON   VALENTINES SERIES

58075

COTON ROAD IN 1907. The new law courts are on the left and the free library on the right.

Old part of Newdegate Arms Hotel Yard

Nunea

THE NEWDEGATE ARMS was an important coaching inn dating back to the sixteenth century. Prior to 1816 it was known as the Black Bull. Until 1895 it also served as the local police court. The grounds behind the inn were extensive and included a sports ground, the local livestock market and stabling for the use of guests.

THE NEWDEGATE ARMS in 1914 with demolition work beginning. The inn was rebuilt further back from the road to allow the widening of Newdegate Square. In 1832 the Riot Act was read from a window of the inn during disturbances on the occasion of the North Warwickshire election. The rioting lasted for two days despite the intervention of the 'Scots Greys'.

THE HOLLYBUSH INN, Bond Gate, c. 1880, before the building of the Prince of Wales (later the Hippodrome) theatre when the two cottages on the left of the picture were demolished.

Bond Gate, Nuneaton

Valentines Series

BOND GATE, early this century. The imposing building on the right is the Conservative Club which was built on the site of the old brewery.

BOND GATE, NUNEATON.

BOND GATE C. 1915. The Hippodrome, with its twin domes, can be seen in the background.

CHURCH STREET. A horse and trap passing by the Marquis of Granby (The Granby Head) on the corner of Bridge Street.

CHURCH STREET, looking towards Attleborough, at the turn of the century.

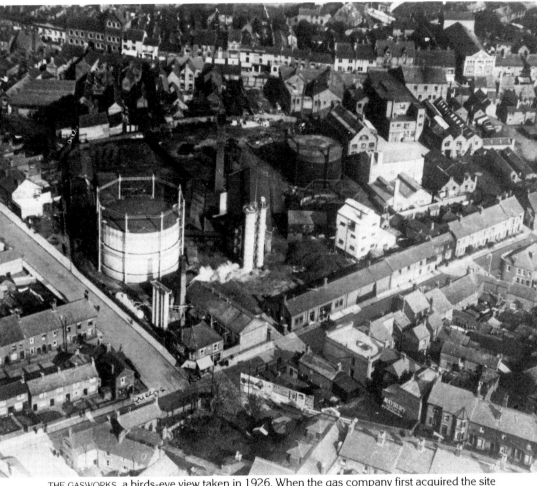

THE GASWORKS, a birds-eye view taken in 1926. When the gas company first acquired the site it paid 3s. a square yard for the land. The site is now Broad Street car-park.

PRINCES STREET in the 1920s.

COTON ROAD, a photograph taken looking towards the town c. 1904.

EDWARD STREET C. 1920.

LANSDOWNE TERRACE, Manor Court Road, a view taken before the First World War. At the time this was regarded as a new suburb of the town.

BRIDGE STREET, COTON, *c.* 1930.

THE OLD WHARFE HOTEL next to the canal bridge on the Coventry Road *c.* 1910.

COVENTRY ROAD looking towards the canal bridge. This photographic study of trees in winter is a reminder of the closeness of the countryside to the town earlier this century.

GRIFF HOLLOWS, on the road to Coventry. The cottage on the left was once a pub called the Newdegate Arms.

GRIFF HOLLOWS, a view along the Griff Arm of the Coventry Canal. This part of the canal was called Red Deeps by George Eliot in her novel *The Mill on the Floss*.

Nuneaton, South Farm Arbury—Birthplace of George Eliot.

SOUTH FARM, ARBURY, at the turn of the century. This was the birthplace of George Eliot (Mary Ann Evans) on 22 November 1819. Her father, Mr Robert Evans, was surveyor and land agent for the Newdegates of Arbury Hall.

Griff House, Nuneaton
(Residence of George Eliot),

GRIFF HOUSE became the home of George Eliot when her family moved from South Farm, Arbury, in 1820. She lived here for twenty-one years. The building is now a Beefeater Steak House.

Nuneaton-Arbury (Cheverel Manor)

W. Cawthorne & Son., Nuneaton. M. C. 1448

ARBURY HALL, the home of the Newdegate family since 1586, was built on the site of Erdbury Priory. Following the Dissolution the priory was demolished and a new house built. In the later eighteenth century the house was converted into a Gothic mansion. George Eliot based both 'Cheverel Manor' and 'Mallinger Abbey' on Arbury.

Old Tea House, Arbury
Nuneaton

THE OLD TEA HOUSE in the grounds of Arbury Hall. One of the many popular postcards produced with George Eliot associations.

AVENUE ROAD (Coton Lane), a view now difficult to imagine, taken c. 1905.

ATTLEBOROUGH, an old thatched pub near the corner of Hall End.

ATTLEBOROUGH HALL, which stood at the junction of Highfield Road and Attleborough Road, was built by a Nuneaton lawyer, George Greenway, in 1809, at a cost of £16,000. The domed structure is the observatory which was added by one of the hall's later owners. This photograph was taken c. 1905; the hall was demolished in 1932.

ATTLEBOROUGH HALL, a gathering on the lawn, probably late last century.

TUTTLE HILL WINDMILL. The mill originally had four sails but a fifth was added in 1906 after a gale had blown one off. A sail blew off again in 1929 and in 1936! At this time the upper part of the mill was pulled down leaving only the stump.

CHAPEL END, the New Inn at the top of Bucks Hill c. 1905. This pub used to be called the Cripples and the junction is still referred to as Cripples Corner by older inhabitants.

CHAPEL END in the 1900s. The Congregational Chapel on the left was built in 1840. It was the work of a fellowship founded by John Dagley, the Stockingford evangelist, in 1807.

CHAPEL END, Ansley Road c. 1905. The shop on the corner is White's Shaving Rooms. Many residents of Chapel End will remember (Jo) Siah White who kept the shop for many years. His brother Jim was also a barber and had a shop at the top of Chapel End.

CAMP HILL HALL, the home of the Stubbs family, in the early 1900s. The hall was demolished in 1939 but the name of the Stubbs family survives locally in 'Stubbs Pool' at the end of Camp Hill Drive.

STOCKINGFORD, Church Road, c. 1905.

LEICESTER ROAD in 1921.

HIGHAM LANE, a view showing a horse and cart disappearing into the distance c. 1920.

HINCKLEY ROAD at the junction with Leicester Road c. 1900. The delivery cart is from the Sunlight Laundry Works at Hinckley.

HINCKLEY ROAD looking towards the railway bridge c. 1900.

HINCKLEY ROAD, a peaceful scene showing two cows and a cart at the turn of the century.

LUTTERWORTH ROAD, NUNEATON

LUTTERWORTH ROAD in the 1920s.

Weddington Hall, Nuneaton

WEDDINGTON HALL early this century. The hall was occupied by the Shawe family from the 1870s until 1923 and was demolished in 1928.

SECTION TWO
Public Services

NUNEATON FIRE BRIGADE demonstrating their equipment. This photograph is undated but was probably taken in the 1890s.

NUNEATON FIRE BRIGADE. This photograph is also undated but is later than the one on the facing page.

THE FREE LIBRARY in Coton Road shortly after it was opened in 1898. It was built at a cost of £2,000 (raised by public subscription) and was later demolished to make way for the new Council House. The library then moved to the old fire station in Queens Road.

THE OLD FIRE STATION and Council offices in Queens Road early this century.

THE NEW COUNCIL HOUSE: a sculptor at work fashioning the columns in 1931.

THE OFFICIAL OPENING of the new Council House in Coton Road on 26 April 1934 by Sir Francis Newdegate.

The New Refuse Destructor at work.

THE CORPORATION REFUSE DESTRUCTOR in St Mary's Road, an undated photograph. Ashes and smoke from the destructor were a constant source of aggravation to the swimming fraternity at the nearby baths. In May 1921 it was noted at the AGM of the swimming club that the ash tip was diminishing slowly. 'Perhaps when we are all dead', added the speaker, 'that tip will have gone.' This remark was greeted with laughter!

ROBINSONS END. Construction of the reinforced concrete reservoir and pumping station in 1903. The contractors were the Yorkshire Henrique Contracting Company from Leeds. At the time the town was experiencing a period of rapid growth and fresh water was in short supply.

THE MARKET PLACE. Work in progress on the main sewerage scheme, 1925–27.

THE BOARD OF HEALTH STEAMROLLER purchased in the mid-1880s for £500. In 1890 it was hired out for 35s. a day.

NEWTOWN ROAD, with the new bridge being tested in 1932. The steamroller on the right looks suspiciously like the one on the facing page.

HARTSHILL SEWAGE WORKS, which were built between 1903 and 1906. In the photograph is Mr Partridge who was the engineer from Fiddian's, the company who supplied the waterwheel-type distribution filters.

THE GENERAL HOSPITAL was opened on 14 September 1893 on land donated by James Tomkinson and Reginald Stanley. Prior to its opening there was no hospital provision in the town. Its construction was largely the result of a lengthy campaign by Dr Nason, a local doctor.

Trade and Industry

SINKING THE CLARA in August 1892 at Griff. The miners were lowered in the bucket which they then filled with spoil by digging beneath their feet. The shaft was named Clara after the daughter of Mrs E.F. Melly.

MINERS WALKING HOME up Whittleford Road from Stanley's Pit (Nuneaton New Colliery). This pit closed in the 1920s.

HAUNCHWOOD COLLIERY, Galley Common, in 1946.

THE COAL STRIKE 1926: picking coal at Griff.

STRIKING MINERS during the 1921 coal strike which started on 1 April and lasted until the end of June. This photograph, and the one below, shows the mining of outcrop coal at Bermuda village by strikers. Fourteen small pits like these were sunk to a depth of about 10ft. and large quantities of coal were worked.

HAUNCHWOOD, the locomotive that bore the colliery's name, photographed in the 1930s.

A GROUP OF MINERS at Dry Bread Colliery, near Chapel End.

Canal Side, New Bridge, Cha...

THE COVENTRY CANAL with the Coventry Road bridge in the background.

VIEW OF THE WINDMILL HILL GRANITE QUARRIES, NUNEATON.

WILLIAM BOON & SONS,

QUARRY PROPRIETORS.

Contractors for Paving, Sewering, Road & Street Construction, &c.,

WINDMILL HILL QUARRIES,   QUEEN VICTORIA ROAD,
Nuneaton.   Coventry.

ALL KINDS OF ROAD MATERIALS.   SAMPLES AND PRICES ON APPLICATION.

NATIONAL TELEPHONE: NUNEATON No. 18; COVENTRY, No. 353.

WINDMILL HILL QUARRY, an advertisement current in 1900 showing the workings.

TUTTLE WHARF, COVENTRY CANAL. A narrow boat belonging to Chas. Mayer of Nuneaton loading stone from Judkins quarry.

HAUNCHWOOD BRICK AND TILE WORKS at Stockingford. An aerial view taken in 1926.

Haunchwood Brick and Tile Co., Ltd., Nuneaton.   Chronicle Series,

HAUNCHWOOD BRICK AND TILE WORKS at Stockingford c. 1904.

TRENT VALLEY STATION. A drawing of the first station on the site which was opened in September 1847.

TRENT VALLEY STATION. The building shown in the picture above was replaced by this one in 1876.

THE MIDLAND RAILWAY STATION (Abbey Street), which was opened in 1864.

1st Dorset Regt. On Strike Duty, Nuneaton Station.

Bradbury Photo

TROOPS ON DUTY at Abbey Street station during the 1911 railway strike.

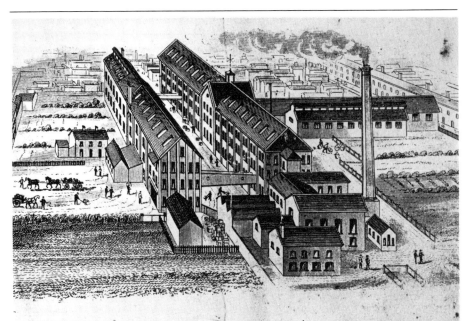

MESSRS. HALL & PHILLIPS, LTD., NUNEATON. BIRD'S EYE VIEW OF THE WORKS.

HALL AND PHILLIPS' HAT FACTORY, Bottrill Street (off Abbey Street), which was opened in 1868 on the site of a disused ribbon factory. This picture shows the extent of the works.

HALL AND PHILLIPS LTD.: the bumping and planking shop. The factory specialised in wool felt hats and fezzes and in 1909 produced 4,000 dozens a week.

HALL AND PHILLIPS LTD.: the finishing shop.

HALL AND PHILLIPS LTD.: the furnaces in 1909.

HALL AND PHILLIPS LTD.: the steaming room in 1909.

THE RELIABLE CLOTHING COMPANY, Queens Road, in 1909. The factory was established in 1892 and produced ready-made clothing, but it also maintained a bespoke service supplying tailors all over the country.

THE RELIABLE CLOTHING COMPANY. A view of the cutting room in 1909.

THE RELIABLE CLOTHING COMPANY: the juvenile clothing machine room 1909. This contained 200 Singer sewing machines and it was said that one competent girl could make 2,500 button-holes a day.

HENRY SLINGSBY AND SONS LTD., Attleborough, manufacturers of regalia, emblematical scarfs, collars, badges, ribbons, banners, etc. Here is the banner-making shop in 1909. This company survived the collapse of the silk ribbon trade by producing a specialised product in demand by Friendly Societies and Trades Unions throughout the country.

HENRY SLINGSBY AND SONS LTD.: the regalia trimming room in 1909.

ANKER MILLS C. 1900. The mill was built as a cotton mill in 1860 by a public subscription company with the intention of alleviating distress in the ribbon trade. This and a subsequent venture failed, and in 1886 the mill was taken over by Fielding & Johnson, becoming a worsted yarn mill, although it continued to be referred to locally as the 'cotton mill'.

NUNEATON OLD BREWERY, which stood between Bridge Street and Newdegate Street, photographed in the late nineteenth century. Production at one point reached 23,000 gallons a week. The brewery was demolished after the lease expired in the 1880s.

DELIVERY CART of Alfred Conner who was based in Fife Street, off Manor Court Road.

THE FLOUR MILL which stood in Mill Walk was built in 1886 by John Knowles. This steam-powered mill was on a site that may well have been used for milling since Domesday.

COOPER'S BAKERY at 50 Queens Road shortly after the new bakehouse was built in the 1920s. William Cooper (on the left) opened the business in 1888 and is shown in this picture with his son George who also worked there. The premises are still a bakery today.

YOXALL'S SHOP, Abbey Street, in 1909. In that year *The Gentleman's Review* reported that: 'Yoxall's Nuneaton Pork Pies are today in constant and regular request all over the world, the counter trade, large as it is, representing only a portion of the demand for them. They are distributed, by the facilities of the Parcel Post, among private consumers in London, the provinces, the Continent, the Colonies, and other places overseas including the Tropics. To their out-of-Britain destinations they are despatched in hermetically-sealed receptacles.'

JOHN RANDLE'S SHOP, Chapel End. An undated photograph. The shop was a bakers and corn dealers but also had a licence to sell beer.

J. PAYNE'S SHOP, the baker and grocer in Croft Road.

SHUTE AND SON'S, the tailors, an early advertisement.

SHUTE AND SON'S SHOP in Queens Road, one of the many retail establishments of the Shute family. Members of the family also had shops in Bond Gate, Coventry Street and the Market Place.

THE MARKET PLACE with market in full swing c. 1910.

FRED GHENT'S HAIRDRESSERS SHOP in Church Street pictured in 1913. The shop was later taken over by Bob Moreton.

SWIFT MOTORS of Stockingford, undated but almost certainly taken in the 1930s.

PARSONS SHERWIN AND CO., New Bridge Street (Newdegate Street) c. 1910. This company combined traditional metalworking with the increasing demand for car sales and repairs.

SAM ROBBINS GARAGE, Leicester Road c. 1909. He also owned a cycle shop in Abbey Street (see p. 19).

SECTION FOUR

People

JOHN BOSWORTH (JACKO), the last town crier of Nuneaton, photographed at the Newdegate Arms sports ground. His uniform was given to him by Harry Pipe, deputy captain of the Fire Brigade and landlord of the Railway Tavern, who had commissioned it for himself when playing Parson Urwin at the Old Theatre. On the skyline of this picture the twin domes of the Hippodrome in Bond Gate can be seen.

FRANCIS ALEXANDER NEWDIGATE NEWDEGATE (1862–1936), MP for Nuneaton from 1892 until 1906. As a resident of Arbury Hall he was the most important local landowner. From 1917 to 1919 he served as Governor of Tasmania.

JOSEPH FIELDING JOHNSON (1840–1917), the first Mayor of Nuneaton 1907–8. Johnson was an entrepreneur who came to the town from Lancashire in 1864 and founded the Nuneaton Wool Company, subsequently renamed the Union Wool & Leather Co. After his second marriage in 1888 to Pattie Townsend, a distinguished artist, he took up residence at Attleborough Hall. He was a founder member of the National Liberal Club.

CORPORAL WILLIAM BEESLEY of Galley Common being awarded his Victoria Cross by King George V for most conspicuous bravery. He was one of two Nuneaton residents to receive the VC, the other being Lieutenant Cecil Knox.

MR HARRY NOON, a waggoner, at Ansley Common c. 1894. The thatched cottage is probably Knight's Farm.

SIR HENRY MADDOCKS KT (1871–1931), Unionist MP for Nuneaton from 1918 until 1923. He was a barrister who subsequently became the City of Birmingham Recorder and was also a member of the Imperial War Graves Commission.

REGINALD STANLEY (1838–1914) was born in Cornwall, educated in Scotland and at the age of 19 went to seek his fortune in the 'wild west' of America. He achieved this by striking gold at Last Chance Gulch in Montana. In 1867 he returned to England and went into the blue brick business with his brother and brother-in-law who were Nuneaton businessmen. His interests expanded, as did his fortune, and he soon established himself as a leading local benefactor. He financed or supported many projects including the new hospital, the Liberal club, the Gate Hotel and several Wesleyan Methodist chapels.

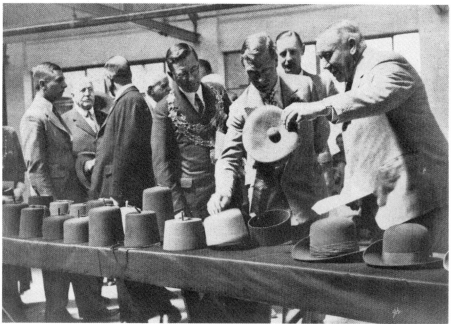

THE ROYAL VISIT of HRH The Prince of Wales to the factory of Hall and Phillips Ltd. on 10 July 1934. Here he is inspecting fezzes destined for use by colonial troops.

MR JOHN WARREN, once a familiar Nuneaton personality. He was often seen riding his tricycle in the town. Before he retired he worked at Anker Mills.

WILLIAM JOHNSON (1849–1919) who served as Lib–Lab MP for Nuneaton from 1906 until 1918. He was Chairman of Bedworth Parish Council from 1894–1910 and a County Councillor. Most significant was his role as General Secretary of the Warwickshire Miners Association.

Church and Chapel

THE WESLEY CHAPEL, Abbey Street c. 1900. This chapel was opened in 1891 and its building was paid for by Reginald Stanley. It replaced an earlier chapel on the same site.

THE CONGREGATIONAL CHURCH BANNER held aloft in a procession along Abbey Street in the 1920s. This was almost certainly 'Treats Day'. The van in the background advertises 'machine carpet beating'.

New. Congregational Church, Nuneaton.

THE NEW CONGREGATIONAL CHURCH in Coton Road shortly after completion in 1904. The former Congregational Church on the same site, built in 1793, can be seen in the aerial view of the town on p. 10 and is also included in the composite view card on p. 15.

THE ABBEY. A very early photograph of the ruins before work was begun on the new St Mary's Abbey Church in 1876.

ST MARY'S ABBEY CHURCH, Manor Court Road c. 1900. Standing among the remains pictured opposite, this church was built as part of a deliberate attempt to reconstruct the plan of the earlier Abbey Church. The foundation stone was laid in 1876 with full masonic honours. Lord Leigh, Right Worshipful Grand Master for Warwickshire, used the same mallet as that used by Charles II to lay the foundation stone for St Paul's Cathedral.

ST NICHOLAS CHURCH c. 1905. On the left can be seen the vicarage and the old grammar school buildings. The school moved to its present site in 1880.

HAYMAKING at the vicarage in 1878.

ST JAMES CHURCH, Weddington, was rebuilt in 1733 following a fire. This view was taken early this century.

STOCKINGFORD CEMETERY in 1920. Note the glass jars; a type of grave furniture no longer used today.

CHILVERS COTON CHURCH C. 1905. The church was seriously damaged by an air attack in May 1941. George Eliot (Mary Ann Evans) was baptised in this church in 1819.

CHILVERS COTON CHURCH. Max Hatzinger, a German prisoner of war, at work sculpting the new font in 1947.

CHILVERS COTON (GEORGE ELIOT'S "SHEPPERTON") PARISH CHURCH REBUILDING APPEAL

Destroyed by bombs 1941: now part rebuilding. £20,000 needed
Donations gratefully received by the Vicar, Chilvers Coton, Nuneaton, Warw's.
Photo. by kindness of Keystone Press Agency, London

CHILVERS COTON CHURCH, the vicar inspects work in progress. The restoration was undertaken largely by German prisoners of war.

CHILVERS COTON CHURCH BELLS standing beside the church wall before being sent for recasting in 1907.

CHILVERS COTON CHURCH NEW BELLS, a photograph taken at John Taylor & Co., the bellfounders in Loughborough. The original three bells were recast and became the fourth, fifth and sixth of the new set of eight.

THE CONGREGATIONAL CHURCH, Chapel End, decorated for Harvest Festival in 1921. The minister is the Revd Trehearne.

THE SALVATION ARMY Life Saving Guard Troop in 1921. Pearl Taylor is holding the flag. This was the Salvation Army's version of the scout movement and the youngest members were known as the Sunbeams. They were merged with the Baden-Powell movement in 1959.

THE SALVATION ARMY BAND on Easter Monday 1907.

THE SALVATION ARMY BAND C. 1892. The original band had just five members. 14 November 1888 was the date of the founding of the Nuneaton Corps and for the first twenty years of its existence it led a very unsettled life, being unable to acquire secure premises. In those early years the Salvationists were often regarded as potential trouble-makers with their tendency to parade and hold noisy public meetings.

Place, Nuneaton. (On Sunday School Festival Day)

SUNDAY SCHOOL FESTIVAL DAY was held at Whitsun. Fine weather brought crowds to the Market Place for this event this particular year. This photograph is undated but is post-marked 1904.

Celebrations and Events

THE MARKET PLACE decorated for Charter Day in 1907. The building on the right is the Birmingham & District Counties Bank which was built by Mr T. Smith of Coton Road, proprietor of the Attleborough stone quarry and brick works.

THE MARKET PLACE decorated for Charter Day: another view.

JACKO, NUNEATON'S LAST TOWN CRIER, at the junction of Edward Street and Queens Road on Charter Day 1907. Paxton's dairy on the corner advertises cream separated new milk at 1½d. a pint.

REGINALD STANLEY'S CAR decorated for the Charter Day festivities in 1907.

ABBEY STREET SCHOOL'S FLOAT for Charter Day 1907. It was entitled 'A Peep in Fairyland'.

JUDKINS QUARRY'S entry for the Charter Day festivities 1907.

CHARTER DAY 1907. The former importance of hand-loom weaving in the town is recalled by this entry in the parade.

GENERAL AND LADY REDVERS BULLER *en route* to the unveiling of the Boer War Memorial in Bond Gate on 28 January 1905. General Buller was a hero of the Boer War having conducted the relief of Ladysmith and expelled the Boer army from Natal.

THE NUNEATON AND HINCKLEY VOLUNTEERS who were part of the procession.

GENERAL BULLER UNVEILING THE WAR MEMORIAL AT NUNEATON,
JAN. 28th, 1905.

THE UNVEILING OF THE BOER WAR MEMORIAL. Large crowds turned out to watch.

THE FLOUR MILLS. This undated photograph shows a delivery vehicle from Nuneaton Flour Mills trimmed up for a special event. The advertisement on the side urges us to buy All-English (National Mark) Flour.

CROWDS OUTSIDE BOB MORETON'S BARBERS SHOP in Coton Road for a special event (alas! unknown) early this century.

A CARNIVAL FLOAT in Abbey Street in the 1930s. The interesting timber-framed building in the background was unfortunately demolished in the 1950s.

THE 1892 ELECTION – crowds in the Market Place await the result. The seat was won by Sir Francis Newdegate (Unionist) with a majority of 641. This view was transformed a few years later by the erection of the Midland & Counties Bank on the corner of Coton Road (see p. 114).

A STEAMROLLER CRASHES into the Old Hollybush at the junction of Leicester Road and Bond
Gate c. 1905. The steamroller driver was a Mr Pearson who lived in Oaston Road.

THE GREAT FLOOD, 30–31 December 1900. The view along Bridge Street.

THE FLOOD, May 1932. During this flood the water in the Market Place reached a depth of 5ft. The floating objects are the wooden blocks that made up the road surface.

THE FLOOD, May 1932, an unusual form of transport in Church Street.

THE FLOOD, May 1932. The scene outside the old Post Office in the Market Place.

THE FLOOD, May 1932. The view inside the Post Office.

A BURST WATERMAIN in Coton Road near the corner of Princes Street in the 1930s.

THE PROCLAMATION OF KING GEORGE V on 10 May 1910 in the Market Place.

THE CORONATION OF KING GEORGE VI in 1937. The decorations at the Palace Cinema by night.

THE BIG FREEZE 1907. A canal scene with school children watching ice-breaking close to Hartshill.

RIVERSLEY PARK — digging a shelter in preparation for war.

BOMB DAMAGE in Church Street. Dozens of bombs were dropped on the town on 16 May 1941 and the damage was extensive.

THE RESCUE SERVICE TEAM 1939–45. Two of these men were awarded the British Empire Medal.

A ST JOHN AMBULANCE EXHIBITION during the early years of the Second World War, demonstrating rescue and decontamination techniques.

NURSES AND MEDICAL STAFF photographed after the exhibition (above).

SECTION SEVEN

Education

KING EDWARD VI SCHOOL. A view of the new buildings in 1880. They replaced the old buildings which can still be seen in St Nicholas' churchyard.

KING EDWARD VI SCHOOL FOOTBALL TEAM c. 1900. Football was dropped from school sports in 1921 and did not return until the school's conversion to a sixth-form college in 1974.

KING EDWARD VI SCHOOL. The school photograph c. 1900. The headmaster at the time was the Revd S. Waters.

FIRST XV, 1933.

Standing—S. R. Moore.   J. Wilson.   H. W. Green.   B. W. Beasley.   C. S. Hawkes.   N. G. Marshall.   W. F. Cummins.   W. H. M. Branston, Esq.

Seated—C. Forshaw.   H. Davies.   F. Gonge.   C. T. Bloxham.   L. F. Bennett.   F. H. Shilton.   R. W. Bircher.

PLAYED 11.   WON 10.   LOST 1.   POINTS : For 293.   Against 31.

KING EDWARD VI SCHOOL FIRST XV in 1933 lost only one match that season. Only fourteen of the fifteen are present in photograph.

KING EDWARD SIXTH SCHOOL CRICKET XI c. 1900. The team were, back row: Caulson, Stewart, Hamilton, Iliffe and Whitehouse; middle row: Lilley, Wright, Stone and Fowler; front row: Ding and Shepheard.

KING EDWARD VI SCHOOL, the chemistry laboratory before the major alterations of 1959.

HARTSHILL SOUTH SCHOOL, class 1A in 1919.

ABBEY STREET SCHOOL: a classroom scene c. 1905.

ABBEY STREET SCHOOL. The staff c. 1905.

ABBEY STREET SCHOOL. The children maypole dancing c. 1905.

ABBEY STREET SCHOOL cricketers c. 1905.

ATTLEBOROUGH SCHOOLS C. 1904. The schools were founded in 1849. In 1906 a teacher called Miss Coleman expressed a desire to remain on the staff after her forthcoming marriage. This was refused by the school managers as unthinkable.

STOCKINGFORD COUNCIL SCHOOL. The 1928–9 netball team after winning the shield.

The Atherstone, Hinckley and Nuneaton Teachers' Association at Monks Kirby, July 9th, 1904.
Baxter's Photo Series. No.

ATHERSTONE, HINCKLEY AND NUNEATON TEACHERS' ASSOCIATION enjoying an outing to Monks Kirby on 9 July 1904.

NUNEATON HIGH SCHOOL FOR GIRLS opened as a County Council supported fee-paying grammar school for girls in 1910. It was the first school in the town to offer secondary education to girls. Pupils in 1910 numbered 110 and the first headmistress was Miss Tanner.

NUNEATON HIGH SCHOOL FOR GIRLS demonstrating the full range of equipment in the gym in 1953.

NUNEATON HIGH SCHOOL FOR GIRLS on the boat at Flushing (The Netherlands) Easter 1939. This school trip was nearly abandoned at the last moment due to the crisis following Mussolini's invasion of Albania on Good Friday.

NUNEATON HIGH SCHOOL FOR GIRLS. The old girls cricket XI during a match in the late 1930s.

THE ELMS SCHOOL-HOUSE in Vicarage Street. The building was damaged in the 1941 air raid and finally demolished in 1960 for road widening. George Eliot became a pupil at this school at the age of seven in 1827 when it belonged to Mrs Wallington.

SECTION EIGHT

Sport and Entertainment

JC PORTE IN HIS AEROPLANE. NUNEATON JULY 12-13-1912. PHO: CARTER.

AN AVIATION MEETING AND GRAND FÊTE in July 1912 at the Weddington Lane cricket ground. The main attraction for a crowd of several thousands was to have been the appearance of M. Moineau, the famous French military aviator, who was engaged to give a series of flights of the Breguet biplane. However, the ministry would not allow him to participate as the aeroplane was still undergoing tests and offered instead Lt. Cyril Porte RN as a substitute, flying a Duperdussin monoplane. It seems that luck was not on the organisers' side as bad weather prevented any flying on the first day and limited it to 20 minutes on the second.

THE WARWICKSHIRE AGRICULTURAL SOCIETY'S SHOW AT NUNEATON AUGUST 29TH 1906. J. WHEELER'S PHOTO. ENFIELD

SHOW JUMPING at the Warwickshire Agricultural Society's show in August 1906 which was held at the Newdegate Arms sports ground. The show was held over two days and tickets were at the rate of six for 10s. Special trains were laid on for the event and the area of the ground was reported to be thronged with people for the two days.

HAUNCHWOOD INSTITUTE BOWLING CLUB, Galley Common, in 1914.

NUNEATON TOWN AFC, the successful team of 1913–14 which won the Birmingham Combination League Shield.

ST MARY'S ROAD OPEN-AIR BATHS: a group of happy bathers in the mid-1920s.

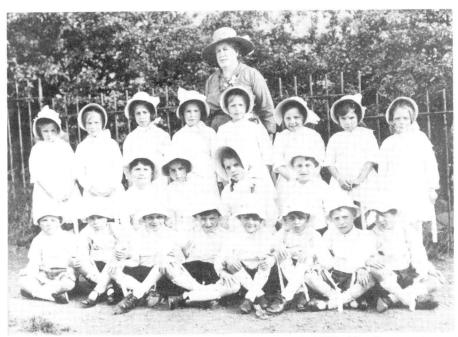

MISS DAVENPORT and her dancing class at Hartshill in the early 1920s. Miss Davenport was a teacher at Hartshill School.

NUNEATON HARRIERS in the 1920s.

THE PALACE CINEMA in Queens Road on the occasion of the coronation of George VI in 1937.
The poster shows that the film that week was 'Poor Little Rich Girl' starring Shirley Temple.

THE

PALACE GARDENS

WORKING MEN'S CLUB.

Victoria Street and Arbury Road. Nuneaton.

THE CLUB is splendidly situated, being in the centre of the Town, and is admirably suited for the purpose for which it is required. The building has provided for all the luxuries of a first-class Club, consisting of a large

Concert, Lecture, and Ball Room,

Also READING, SMOKING, and BILLIARD ROOMS, fitted up on the latest lines. The whole of the building is fitted up with the Electric Light.

Adjoining the Club are ORNAMENTAL GROUNDS, which should be appreciated by the Members. At the rear of the premises it is intended to provide outdoor games, such as QUOITS, SKITTLE ALLEY, &c.

Should the Committee be able to secure more land, they intend making a BOWLING GREEN. These extensions will make the Club one of the finest in the Midlands.

Intending Members may now join by paying their Subscription to the

SECRETARY

PALACE GARDENS, NUNEATON.

THE PALACE GARDENS WORKING MEN'S CLUB. The ornamental grounds mentioned in the advertisement later became the site of the Palace Cinema. They can be seen in the foreground of the aerial view on p. 29.

NUNEATON CINEMA PROPRIETORS AND MANAGERS in the 1930s. At this time there were nine cinemas in the town, six of which were in the town centre: the Royal, the Scala, the Hippodrome (formerly the Prince of Wales), the New Palace, the Ritz and the Princes. Attleborough, Stockingford and Chapel End could also boast local cinemas.

THE PRINCE OF WALES THEATRE (later the Hippodrome) in Bond Gate: a photograph taken shortly after its opening in 1900. It was closed in the mid-1950s and eventually destroyed by fire in 1968. The statue of Euterpe was manufactured in Stanley's brickyard and is now in the entrance of the Riversley Park Museum.

ROYAL :: Perfect Pictures

ROYAL ELECTRIC HALL, STRATFORD STREET, NUNEATON.

The LATEST LIVING PICTURES & HIGH-CLASS VARIETY.

7 TWICE NIGHTLY **9**

Sole Proprietor:
E. A. SHUTE.

Manager:
J H. PHILLIPS.

:: TELEPHONE 5yl. ::

THE ROYAL ELECTRIC HALL, Stratford Street; the first cinema in the town. It was opened c. 1909.

RIVERSLEY PARK. Dredging the river Anker in the early 1900s. This card is undated but is almost certainly a view of the operations to deepen and widen the river at the time that the park was laid out. The Pingles embankment can be seen in the background.

RIVERSLEY PARK, a view from the Pingles embankment soon after its completion in 1907. It was built on land given by Alderman Melly. The Union Wool & Leather Company works are the buildings on the right. The museum was still to be built.

RIVERSLEY PARK, another view taken shortly after its opening in 1907.

HEATH END AFC 1921–22.

NUNEATON BOROUGH SILVER PRIZE BAND pictured outside the new Council buildings probably in 1934.

JACKO WITH THE FIRST GATE PRIZE at the Sam Robbins' sponsored sports at the Newdegate Arms sports ground. This, and the following photograph, were taken in the hotel yard. Sam Robbins was the proprietor of a garage in Leicester Road (see p. 88), and a cycle shop in Abbey Street (see p. 19).

THE SECOND GATE PRIZE at the Sam Robbins' sponsored sports. A valueless donkey!

ACKNOWLEDGEMENTS

The authors wish to express their sincere thanks to the following for their kind and thoughtful assistance. Mr J. Burton, Mr & Mrs A. Clews, Mr & Mrs T. Farmer, Mr W. Harding, Mr P. Lee, Mrs E. Owen, Mrs Pym, Mrs E. Richardson, Mrs N. Savage, Miss A. Robson and the staff of the Nuneaton Art Gallery and Museum, Etone School, King Edward VI Sixth Form College, Nuneaton and Bedworth Borough Council and Warwickshire County Record Office.